Modern
CTO

Joel Beasley

Modern CTO Press
7365 Merchant Court #3
Sarasota, FL 34240
http://moderncto.io
hello@moderncto.io

Ordering Information:
Quantity sales. Special discounts are available on quantity purchases by corporations, associations, and others. For details, contact the publisher at the address above.

CONTENTS

Modern
CTO

PREFACE

set out to write this book to share what I learned going from developer to CTO. I thought this path and my experience were the exception. Although I did know a handful of developers who became CTOs, I had an overwhelming image in my head that the majority of CTOs were corporate giant *IT types*.

I looked in the CTO section of Amazon's bookstore, and it was bare with nothing recent or useful. All that was there were a few corporate-giant-feeling books and white papers on Google on "The scientific analysis of CTOs in 1999." It all felt very old guard—not my style.

Having gone from developer to CTO, I estimated that maybe 10-20% of all CTOs were originally developers. I ran a Facebook ad for potential readers to pre-register for this book and was overwhelmed by the number of CTOs who registered from all over the world. Are there really this many of us?

BIRTH OF THE PODCAST

I started sharing the half-baked chapters of this book with the CTOs I knew. This generated some excellent discussions that I started to record and share with Lead Developers and CTO friends. They said, "You should put these online and make a podcast out of them." So I did and the *Modern CTO Podcast* was born.

When the open guest spots outnumbered the people I knew, I began looking up each CTO that registered for this book. One by one, over the course of three weeks, I emailed each person individually inviting them to come on the podcast to share their experiences and help pull up the next generation of technologists.

There were only two types of responses from the CTOs I reached out to. The first was, "Yes, would love to." The second was, "I don't believe I would have anything useful to share. I had an atypical experience as I went from developer to CTO." And there it was. Day after day, more and more people responded in these two ways. My friends, there are more of us that you can imagine.

60-80% OF CTOs ARE DEVELOPER TO CTO

I was shocked when I found out that the majority of CTOs on the planet today went from developer to CTO. I'm not alone! Woo! Here I was thinking that I was rare on this pale blue dot, all while being surrounded by others who had the same experience. It was like finding a place where you fit-in and belong.

Why hadn't anyone else been speaking up? Probably because we were all busy building empires and executing future plans. However, there is value to be had in reflecting on and sharing our experiences; value that can help us more effectively move forward in our pursuits.

THE SPACE BETWEEN

In music, you find beauty in the space between the notes. If you heard all the notes at once, it would sound like a piano hitting the ground—not pretty. It's true in fine art as well; the beauty is in the space between the objects. And in life, the beauty is in time, the space between here and not here. The 0 and the 1.

Developer and CTO are two distinct roles. It's the experience of transitioning the space between them that is unique to our generation. Navigating the path of this new transition between developer and CTO roles successfully is jagged and sometimes difficult. And it should be, right? This is our first time experiencing a technology revolution. No one is great at anything on the first try. We basically all just pioneered and dealt with this together. We need to take a breath, recalibrate, and share what we know with the next generation.

SMOOTH THE JAGGED EDGES

We have an incredible opportunity for growth in virtually every aspect of our role. Every skill we learned on this path from developer to CTO defines the Modern CTO. These skills were not handed to us; we had to discover and earn them. We developed skills in: relationships, growth, communicating value, scaling, management, learning how to learn, balancing imbalance, opportunity, focus, identifying white space, understanding failure, processing feedback, making people feel heard, sharing, speaking up, teaching, and developing effective products that bring value to the market.

We are acutely aware of these skills because we had to consciously learn them as adults and intentionally put effort into bettering ourselves. It didn't just happen by chance. You put in the work; you get the results.

We have a library of skills, each with battle scars with stories to tell. And while we can't put in the work for the next generation, we *can* hand them a map when all we had were the nighttime stars.

IT'S ALL FOR YOU

It was like I had been looking my whole life for a place where I fit-in, belonged, and could bring value. Then one day, walking out to my car after talking to multiple CTOs, learning and sharing all day with the brightest minds on the planet, I just knew. This is what I wanted out of life: to share, to help, and to bring up the next generation of technology leaders.

This isn't *my* podcast or book. This is *ours*. I'm incredibly grateful that I get to be a part of what is happening.

Thank you.
Joel

ARE YOU
A VISIONARY CTO?

"**A**m I a visionary CTO?" I was asked this question when editing the book, and I didn't really know how to respond. I feel like I understand Visionary CTOs, and I may have some of their characteristics.

Successful people are often driven by something that happened to them early in life. Both Elon Musk and Jeff Bezos had it really rough growing up. Elon had an abusive father, and Jeff's mom was 16 years old when he was born. Or, take Gary Vaynerchuk who came to the US as a poor immigrant and had to split two-ply toilet paper to conserve resources.

For these men, living through those trials somehow translated into a relentless drive to not only to be creative but to see their vision come to fruition. They have a deep understanding of what it means to struggle. Being a visionary is nothing magical. It's more like an ungodly persistence. It's a skill learned out of necessity.

BORED AT WORK

Back when I was a kid, my dad took me to work with him every weekend to give my mom a break. I sat there, every Saturday and Sunday for months on end, bored out of my mind, staring at computers. I can still remember the smell and the taste in the air sitting in that vast empty office. Perhaps out of sheer boredom, I got a taste for programming at the age of 10.

LEARNING TO WALK AGAIN

When I was 13 years old I got hit by a car. Halfway through my initial recovery, I fell and broke even more bones. It's hard to describe how difficult it was for me. I had people bathing me and helping me on the toilet during my adolescence. Talk about humiliating. I fell into depression and my weight ballooned up to 300 pounds—all this by the age of 16.

I was taken out of school for about a year and basically spent all day programming. At one point, I tried to set-up a meal delivery service since I was at home all day and I wanted food. I tried to get a credit card processor, but I couldn't because I was too young. I remember with my broken bones, crawling up the stairs backward after getting pizza delivered. Eventually, the pizza guy just came into the house and up to my room since I ordered out so much. That's how I ended up gaining so much weight.

In order to process payments, I needed a bank account. The only way to do this online was through PayPal. Despite my best efforts, the business never got off the ground. Still, during this exploration, I discovered I could make money online as a freelance code writer. When I began getting account summaries in the mail, my parents freaked. They thought for sure I was involved in some illegal hacking scheme.

Eventually I got fed up with being overweight, and I decided to engage in the struggle. I began to exercise, lose weight, and regain my dignity. I had to pull myself up more than once—having to go to school in a wheelchair, learning to walk again, getting into shape—all of it taught me to dig deep and to get up again.

Then, I decided I wanted to quit school. We met with the principal, and I laid it all out for him. I was making money, and I knew I wanted to program for the rest of my life. We shook hands, and he let me graduate through the early exit program. By the time I was 17 years old I was a full time programmer, and by age 18 I sold my first technology for $1 million.

I strived to be the *best programmer ever*. Still, it wasn't long before I saw that, when you get to be in the top tier of programmers, everyone just argues. I also realized that my income as a programmer was limited. After selling my technology, I got exposed to the business side of things. I began to ask, "Is there a programmer that's also a business person?" That's the CTO.

KNOW YOURSELF

When you're trying to get your atrophied limbs to start working again, you pay a lot of attention to your body. My self-awareness became highly developed. There was a lot of self-reflection back then—I *had* to be aware. Somehow, I've been able to transfer this self-awareness into the business realm, and I keenly recognize my strengths and weaknesses. If I can't do it, I get the best person that can. I can only know so much and that's fine.

Who hasn't had their share of hardships? I'm sure you've noticed that I'm not selling any get-rich-quick schemes. I've paid my dues, and you will too. It doesn't require huge amounts of suffering to become a visionary. Rather, it requires transforming the obstacles in your life into opportunities. You become stronger and more confident as you get through each trial. So, lift the heaviest cross you can bear and carry it like a champion.

PUSH THROUGH THE PAIN

When I was in a wheelchair, I didn't want to move my legs. They were weak, and I felt intense pain. Still, I had to move if I wanted walk again. I saw that I wanted to walk and did what it took to get back on my feet. In that moment, I was a visionary.

Notice anything strange about this conversation? There's barely even a mention about tech or business strategies. In the broader sense, visionaries typically come out of the backwoods without even a care about our Silicon Valley world. Instead, it's their struggle that defines them and gives birth to their vision.

The essence of being a visionary is not being satisfied with who you are right now, and always, always moving towards who you want to be in the future.

CAN VISIONARY-ISM BE TAUGHT?

Beyond taking stock of your personal story, is it possible to train someone to think like Steve Jobs? Phil McKinney, an innovation consultant and former CTO of HP's $40 billion PC division, seems to think so. His track record includes turning a $1.5 billion loss into a $2 billion profit and claiming the world's top PC maker spot.

McKinney offers some awesome ideas to spur visionary thoughts (like:)

- Change routines (new social circles, new routes to work, new conversations)

- Brainstorm about stuff unrelated to your niche (list 50 ideas about how to start a lawn care service)

- Pay special attention to assumptions and challenge every one of them

McKinney also encourages us to never stop at the first answer. For example, what's half of 13? 6.5, right? Well, in his innovation workshop they came up with 43 different answers. This means the numbers 1 and 3 could be two halves of the written number 13.[1]

Still, you can teach someone to sing, and they may technically do it correctly, but some voices still make us cringe.

BRILLIANT IDEAS AREN'T VISIONARY ENOUGH

It's not enough just to come up with incredible ideas. The visionary CTO must have a high capacity to execute, organize, identify whitespace, communicate, and lead.

Empathy & Visualization

This means developing self-awareness as well as being acutely aware of others. Feel and understand the problem, then visualize the solutions. This could be a people problem or a tech issue. Observe, stop, and think.

Organize & Execute

Gather people, resources, validate experts, and put together the A-team. The B-team gets B results. Hire where you're weak. Know your strengths and double down on them.

IDENTIFY WHITESPACE

Whitespace is existing technology that hasn't yet matured commercially. To blend emerging technology with growing demand requires both technological and business vision. Ask questions like, "Will millions of people be doing this in 24 months?" For example, I believe in 20 years we'll live in a world where virtual reality (VR) is as prominent as social media. Still, I don't see the consumer behavior there yet for me to warrant planning a business around VR in the next 12 to 24 months.

However, as of today, voice is the future. Alexa and Google Home sold out this past holiday season. (I found this out by going into Best Buy and asking the manager what the three most popular items were. He said that there weren't even three items that would top the list, just one, and it was voice.) It was the first time I can remember that the top wish list item of parents and kids was the same thing. Although voice has only penetrated

10% of the US population, it's growing exponentially. Everyone I have spoken to in the business world has said that it's not mature yet. But this is the time to get involved! It's exploding and whoever is there now will be on the top in five years.

COMMUNICATION & LEADERSHIP

Being a leader means communicating complex ideas simply. You've got to make high-level ideas stick in their minds. The easier it is to understand something I make, the more people will spread the word.

In his book, *Start with Why*, Simon Sinek says: "Very few people or companies can clearly articulate WHY they do WHAT they do....By WHY I mean what is your purpose, cause or belief. WHY does your company exist? WHY do you get out of bed every morning? And WHY should anyone care?"[2] It's critical for me to understand what drives people. At its core, it means I care about what matters to them as people, not just as workers. This principle ties back to the empathy concept—what's their *why?* Simon's book forever changed how I think.

Finally, communication appears in many forms, so I have to be really aware. Legendary management consultant Peter Drucker once said, "The most important thing in communication is hearing what isn't said."[3] Silence may actually be a problem screaming for attention.

LIMITED BY YOUR OWN IMAGINATION AND EXECUTION

A large part of being a visionary is fully grasping questions about market viability and consumer behavior. Great ideas are only one of the requirements needed to achieve success at scale. The full visionary formula includes: Vast Topic Expertise + Creative Thinking + Solid Logic + Wisdom Cortex.

I find myself telling younger technologists that you're only limited by your imagination. Act without thinking, and you run in circles; think without acting and you stand still. The trick is in thinking and acting together to move you forward. Imagination and execution together will take you wherever you want to go in life.

WHAT SHOULD A MODERN CTO KNOW?

What are the responsibilities of a CTO? This is the question I hear most often. And the answer is always dependent on the situation. So, how then do you define a Modern CTO? By defining the areas of knowledge the Modern CTO should have. A Modern CTO knows:

- Developers Are Not CTOs
- The Spaghetti Code MVP Epidemic
- Over-Engineering Is a Problem
- How to Create & Destroy Momentum
- Whether to Hire, Buy, or Outbuild Their Competitor
- How Not to Scale Prematurely
- How to Solve Any Problem
- How to Work with Programmers When You Aren't One
- UX Mistakes to Watch Out For
- When to Speak Up
- When to Hire Consultants
- How to Analyze Failure
- How to Bounce Back from Unforeseen Constraints
- Answer the Question: "How Difficult is it to Code…?"
- How to Avoid the "Bottom of the Ninth Guy"
- When to Abandon Ship
- How to Miss a Deadline
- When to Respond to Feedback
- How to Validate an Expert in Any Field
- How to Effectively Communicate Complex Ideas

DEVELOPERS ARE NOT CTOs

1

Developers are not CTOs. I remember an argument I heard from a single developer CTO. He'd say stuff like, "Well I made the product and I was here when it started, so I'm the best fit for CTO." That was me a decade ago. Wow, was I ignorant.

What if we extend that logic to other parts of life? "Well, I was standing next to him when he had a heart attack, and I make medical equipment, so I'm the best one to do the triple bypass." It's laughable. If I rest on past achievements, I'll never grow. Let me put it this way—a genius programmer could be a lousy CTO. On the other hand, a mediocre developer could be a CTO that makes companies millions.

HOLD THE HATE MAIL

This doesn't mean a developer can't learn to be a CTO. It took me over a decade on a tough road of experience, pain, and expense to get there. We're never good at something the first time we try. I'm very experience dependent just like Machine Learning is heavily dependent on a good set of training data. More Data + Higher Quality = Improved Performance.

WAIT, HOW LONG? 17 FRIGGIN' YEARS, REALLY.

It took me about five years to get good at programming and five more to become excellent. And it took me five years to not look like an idiot as a CTO and another five years to become fantastic. That's actually about 20 years.

MIND SHIFT

The shift in thinking from writing code to creating and communicating value didn't come easily for me. What did come easily for me was understanding how people think. I stumbled around for quite a while, about four years. Then over the course of that fifth year these isolated lessons and skills all melded together: how people think, how to create value, how to communicate value, and how to manage people.

PRO TIP: LEVERAGE OTHERS' EXPERIENCE

Books condense a lifetime of experience into a few hours' read. Powerful right? When I was cutting my teeth, there weren't any books or blogs on how to be a Modern CTO. Nobody was out there to point me in the right direction about testing. I have obtained the experience, so maybe something I say can help pull *you* up.

THE SPAGHETTI CODE
MVP EPIDEMIC

2

Early in my career, I wrote my share of horrible code. There's always room to improve. If you keep at it, you eventually end up in a room with other top experts arguing about various methodologies.

PLEASE, STOP THE MADNESS

I've noticed a disturbing new trend or a Malcolm Gladwell-esque epidemic actually. Rather than developers and startup entrepreneurs saying, "We wrote it poorly because we're new and lack experience," they'll say, "We built an MVP." Nope, you've built a MESS.

Ideally I'd snap my fingers and turn everyone into quality programmers instantly, problem solved. Oh well, I guess I'll settle for trying to get the word out about what is *not* an MVP.

NO EXCUSE FOR POOR CODE

A minimal viable product is a heuristic for building only what is needed to carry out the task in the most basic form: MVP + Users + Feedback + Release = Version 1. Notice how nowhere in that equation is fixing a broken spaghetti mess?

PROTOTYPE VS. MVP?

Let's say you were designing a hairbrush. So, you get a block of foam, you cut out the pattern, and then you glue on some bristles. Then, you hand paint it and stick on a handle with some duct tape. That would be a prototype. You could brush your hair with it, but it's not a product ready for market.

To get to an actual product, you'd have to go through a whole other process, which includes detailed design and production steps. A minimal viable product is something you can take to market and sell. The definitions speak for themselves.

- **prototype** - *noun,* a first or preliminary version of a device or vehicle from which other forms are developed

- **minimal** - *adjective,* of a minimum amount, quantity, or degree

- **viable** - *adjective,* capable of working successfully; feasible

- **product** - *noun,* an article or substance that is manufactured or refined for sale

The problem with using prototype and MVP interchangeably is that it generates confusion. When someone improperly assigns the term MVP to a prototype—and they take it to investors —it's probably because they want money or want to expand. They don't know what these terms really mean. Instead of an MVP, they're presenting an unrefined mess, like the foam back hairbrush. Then investors think they can run with it, dump cash into it and take it to market. That's where problems occur because the product is still vastly under-engineered.

I've been called in numerous times by companies saying to me, "Hey, we have this MVP, but we're having problems with it." This happens since they tried to scale it, and they found they only have something that *looks* like a product. They still have to engineer it and answer all the questions required for something to be a product. So I have to tell them, "This isn't a product; it's a prototype."

The definitions above are perfect. A product is something "manufactured or refined for sale." Perfect. It's the refinement process that separates the prototype from the MVP. Getting from prototype to MVP is a lot of work. If you can't take it to market and sell it at scale, it's not a product. If you tried to sell your foam, duct tape hairbrush on QVC, you wouldn't sell a single brush.

GOOD ENOUGH

I don't obsess with trying to make it perfect, but I've learned to be patient and write code that is good enough by expert standards. If you aren't an expert, then your "good enough" is actually poor. The difference between "good enough" for a mid-level developer and an expert is mind boggling.

There are only two reasons you write bad code:

1. You know how to write good code, but choose to write bad code.

2. You don't know how to write good code.

And both suck.

OWN YOUR MESS

If you rushed something out on the cheap in order to get a proof of concept and raise money, that's understandable. I get it. But, when you raise money, make sure to ask for enough to do the project right and with a stellar team. If you aren't sure how much is enough, reach out to me. You want to form a team that delivers a Fortune 500-level product that doesn't need to be rewritten.

You only get one shot with someone else's money. If the business side doesn't work out, so be it. But, if you delivered a quality product, your reputation grows and more opportunities will come your way. If you build a lousy, unstable product, and the business limps along or fails—all fingers point at you.

OVER-ENGINEERING IS A PROBLEM

3

THE HIDDEN CANCER IN YOUR TECH TEAMS

Sometimes we nerds are just too strict. This shows up all the time in development teams. Over-engineering the process or project creates unnecessary clutter in your pipeline. It's natural to create systems and get emotionally attached to them, but, if left unchecked, this grows like a cancer in your organization. I'm wary of engineers competing for system and process creation based on what's trendy and not what best meets business goals.

IT DOESN'T DO ANYTHING FOR ANYONE BUT YOU

There's a now famous email that Elon Musk once sent out to his SpaceX team. The subject line was: Acronyms Seriously Suck. Basically, he blasted them for making up unnecessary acronyms that confuse communication, especially for new hires. Elon wrote, "VTS-3 is four syllables compared with 'Tripod,' which is two, so the bloody acronym version actually takes longer to say than the name!"[4] So, if it's a wheel, call it a wheel for heaven's sake.

GOOD ENOUGH IS BETTER THAN PERFECT

Bill Nye *is* the science guy, and I grew up with him as a kid. He did science experiments on TV, and all the kids would watch him in school. Bill wrote this book[5] where he talks about DNA progression and how animals and species change. Why are there five fingered vs. four fingered animals? What's the difference? Well, they adapt to survive. It's a very slow process and species can diverge greatly.

You don't have to be the sexiest male. You don't have to be the most fertile. You can't be the least fertile, either. You don't have to be the best, but you can't be the worst. You only have to be good enough to get to the next generation. My DNA only has to be good enough to survive long enough to replicate. If I survive long enough to replicate, I'm good enough to get to the next successive generation. People preach perfection, but the reality is your business only has to be good enough to stay in business that year. If your business is always good enough to stay in business that year, then you're always in business.

You might say, "Oh, I want the perfect user experience." But really, you only need something good enough for someone to use it. Get a hundred people to use it, and then improve it. Then get a thousand people to use it, and improve it again. It doesn't have to be perfect. It has to be good enough, and then move forward from there. If you reiterate internally too many times, you negotiate against yourself. So get it out the door already.

This is not an excuse to *not* strive for excellence. I'm not going to be lazy and write a bunch of spaghetti code. "Good enough" is a reasoning that I use to allow myself to advance. If I'm obsessing over making something perfect, I have two choices: I can dump three more hours into it or move on. I can remember that even my DNA and the universe are only "good enough." I use that to allow myself to let it go.

COMBAT OVER-ENGINEERING WITH FOCUS ON THE VALUE

It's imperative for me to constantly pull the business objectives back into view and remind us about the "why." Take the focus off the process, and place it on the value. Injecting business focus into your daily standup meetings avoids the natural tendency to get caught-up in the details. By continuously bringing the business into the conversation, I eliminate over-engineering and drive momentum instead.

Problems appear all too frequently in the name of "efficiency" or "optimization." When I see this, I immediately tell people to stop thinking in terms of adding value to the platform. Instead, think of how to add value to the customer.

FEAR-BASED FEATURES ARE A PROBLEM

When you build a feature out of fear of losing the customer *instead* of building it out of value to the customer, you have built a fear-based feature. I find that newer companies often have this problem. It happens most often as a knee-jerk reaction to criticism on new projects. You get feedback from a few users, and you rush out to fix things out of fear of losing their attention. You aren't building for one person; you are building for a market. Dive too deeply on one individual's desire and you'll end up with an app only one person cares to use. You can avoid this mistake by knowing how to process feedback which I go over in Chapter 18: When to Respond to Feedback.

HOW TO CREATE
& DESTROY MOMENTUM

4

n my experience, momentum has been the single biggest reason a project flops or flies. All of the most successful and effective leaders I've met have this uncanny ability to create momentum within their teams and organizations. You might not be surprised to learn I'm a big fan of Simon Sinek since the guy always talks about leaders and motivation and why people do things.

NOT ROCKET SCIENCE, BUT DON'T TRY TO FLY WITHOUT IT

It's pretty basic if you think about it. Momentum is simply the rate at which you accomplish your goals. Not all goals are created equal. It's not just coming up with the goals; it's about getting buy-in and ownership from the individuals that will be executing the goals—that's the soul of momentum.

Your ability to clearly communicate why something is important is critical to success. The *why* is the foundation of momentum. Why are we here? Why are we waking up every day and working together on this project? What's the point? This why is much easier to understand and to take ownership of when it's broken down into more digestible pieces. I'll explain exactly how to do this later.

When I create a new team or join an existing team, the initial momentum may be zero or even at a negative. Typically, when I come in, there isn't a large forward impetus that I'm joining. Instead, there's a situation or a problem with a distinct lack of energy. If an organization or situation already has inertia, I focus on injecting value into the mix. In most cases, this is easier because I just hit the ground and run with everyone else. For an organization that's spinning its wheels though, it's much harder. You have to rally the troops and build up an entire momentum framework.

Creating momentum from nothing

When I first meet a team, I like to get to know the group and then meet everyone one-on-one. It's important to establish a very simple, basic relationship with them. I try to put them at ease from the beginning. It's not about trying to be their best friend or anything like that. Still, I want to know one or two interesting things that drive them as individuals and to share with them why I'm doing what I'm doing.

I take notes when we meet. This way I can remember that John likes vacations in the mountains and Beth brews her own beer. There's nothing disingenuous about this. I just simply can't remember everything I would like to, so I take notes and review them regularly.

One thing I strive to provide the team is direct access to me. I don't ignore the chain of command, but I take the initiative to reach out on a personal level. There's nothing more reassuring than knowing that the leader knows who I am and what's important to me. The greater the distance a person feels from the top tier, the less they feel a part of the team.

Also, the worst thing for any team is a losing streak. No matter how great the individuals may be as developers or people, a losing team loses hope. For this reason, I set the pace with a sequence of small—nearly guaranteed—wins that lead us to eventual bigger victories. This is how I create momentum, even at a place that appears dead.

BREAK IT DOWN, LIKE ELON MUSK

I like to apply Elon Musk's "First Principles Thinking" approach which he borrows from physics. It basically states that you work backward from the source instead of reasoning from analogy.[6]

Look at Tesla cars. For years, everybody thought electric cars weren't viable. They said, "No, it's too expensive. The batteries are too expensive, so we're not going to make electric cars." And so they would say, "Lexus tried it; others tried it. It didn't sell because it was so expensive, so we're not going to do it."

Well, Elon says that instead of using prior failure as scientific proof, he asks, "Why didn't it work for them?" Well, it didn't work because of cost. So, how much did everything cost? Okay well, all these components cost this, and the batteries cost that.

Elon discovered that the batteries were outrageously overpriced, and there wasn't a great reason why. Materials were cheap on the London exchange, and the costs to put batteries together were significantly less than what they were selling for. Margins were high, and this presented an opportunity. So he bought the materials, built them himself, and Tesla was born.

First Principles aren't just for Elon, or physicists. I use this in my everyday life and in my business. I always seek the *why*. It reveals the root, and from there we see if everything adds up. If it does, great; it makes sense. If not, there's usually an opportunity present.

Here's how I might do it: I could start by deciding that the first milestone is our first customer. To understand how to land the first customer though, we need to work backwards. It means we need a product, a message, and we need to communicate that message.

So, the central truth I establish is reaching the first milestone (Customer #1). Then, working in reverse, I ask, "What are the basic fundamentals I need in order to make that sale?" Well, I need a product or service, and I need a message that I'm going to communicate about the product or service. Plus, I need a method to communicate my message. And that's it. That's how I establish the initial milestones and the subsequent supporting goals.

MOMENTUM IS EXPONENTIAL

Humans think linearly, but momentum is exponential. It's hard for our minds to imagine exponentially, but this vision is critical for the Modern CTO. It helps you stay focused and keeps your team motivated. Exponential vision means you see that a series of small goals will fulfill milestones, and a series of milestones will lead to explosive growth.

Before you know it, you're sitting on a massive hundred-million-dollar organization—seriously. Still, the only way we can get there is by taking the basic first principles and repeating them over and over again. You build momentum, and that momentum eventually gets magnified exponentially.

Destroying momentum

You can stop twice as fast as you can accelerate. I'm sure you've experienced this when you try to change lanes—it's much easier to slow down and fall behind than it is to accelerate and get ahead. Still, it's a serious amount of fun to put the hammer down and pass! In the context of team momentum. It's also true that you can stop twice as fast as you can speed up. You can destroy momentum in an instant.

ARTIFICIAL MOMENTUM

I'll often see companies that get huge injections of capital and start spending the money on bringing people in, opening offices, and all that stuff.

They're not spending their money like they're poor. They create artificial momentum through investment capital, and that's something to watch out for. It isn't good when you get investors to inject capital, and you create a lot of buzz, but your buzz isn't creating lasting value.

So, if I get $250,000 from an investor, I have to make super sure that every dollar I spend of that money is like I'm spending my own last $250,000. I have to generate value. I see so many companies just trying to get to the next round of investments. It's really bad. I see it happen on a daily basis, and it kind of scares me because I don't know how much is happening outside of projects that I'm a part of. I see these CEOs and these founders wasting money. They get a lot of money, and they blow through it. Then they're sitting there, and they need more investment money because they have a $40,000 a month payroll with $5,000 a month in revenues. There's just no discipline.

Artificial momentum and lack of discipline are things that will cripple the organization. So watch out. When you get that money, you don't need a $500 coffee maker for the office, right? If you go over to a new country, *immigrant-style,* you try to hustle and start it up. You don't need a $500 coffee maker, so you make sure that you only spend money on what you need.

A lot of strong companies never even take investment capital. They just don't. These guys use their first contract from their first clients, take that profit and reinvest it back in their business.

Last night my wife brought over a small Christmas tree to my new office, a five-foot-tall artificial Christmas tree. She goes, "You know, I just got this as a present for you to congratulate you on the new office." In my head, though, I'm thinking, we don't need a Christmas tree, right? We could spend $60 on advertising or use it to create further value. We could've reached a thousand people with 60 bucks. That's a thousand more people I could've helped with my information, but she spent it on a Christmas tree that only three or four people will ever even see.

Well, the husband side of me said, "That was so sweet! Thank you so much!" and I gave her a big hug.

That night, I lay in bed wondering if there were any way I could secretly return the tree. It wasn't because I was broke. It's just the mentality I try to have. What's my minimally valuable business? I'm playing the long game; I'm playing the decade here.

The reason I do this is because I've screwed up in the past. I wasted the money. I made the mistakes and it sucked. It was horrible, and I already did my Rocky Round II coming back up thing, but I'm never, ever going back. That lesson was learned with a lot of pain, and I will never repeat it again. And that's kind of where I am with artificial momentum. When I see people taking investment money, it scares me. I just want to reach out and say, "I'm glad you got your investment money. Just don't do what I did the first time I got money, 'cause I screwed up."

STACK THE TOWELS

Another way to destroy momentum is to have people redo stuff. If you have people constantly having to redo the same thing, it's the quickest way to destroy momentum. Let's say you're in a retail store, and you pay someone to fold towels. Then, you walk right over to them after they finish, and you knock the towels over. They have to refold the towels. You do that a couple of times, and they're going to quit.

The same thing happens with programming and developing products. If you keep having your team rebuild and refold, only to walk over and smack it down, they are going to quit. It's not about money at that point; it's about momentum. I've seen managers make a feature change, and they don't even tell the developers across the room. So, you've got developers burning cash, building something that will never be used, and managers that just let them finish it.

Things like this happen in organizations that are not super planned. If you're in a situation like this right now, and you've got people working on something that you know will not be used, just do them a favor and stop them. Just go stop it. No one wants to feel like their work is useless.

Maybe you're in a situation, and you can't stop it. You still have options. You can walk over there and say, "Great, good job, yep, alright. Now you can throw that away because we're never going to use that again." Say that, and you've just made that person feel worthless. You made them feel horrible because they just wasted time in their life, and we only have a limited amount of time in our lives.

No one at my business or at my company will ever feel like the work they did was useless. I may not use it, but I'm never saying, "Nope, it's useless; we're never going to use it." If you find yourself saying that, it will kill your team's momentum.

If I have situation where someone just finished something that we've decided we're not going to use, I'll communicate it in a way that doesn't make them feel useless. I might say, "Awesome, great work; this is fantastic. We're going to put this in the roadmap here to go ahead and move it into this future branch. High Five, great job." That's an entirely different conversation than saying, "Oh, yeah, they've decided they didn't want it; it's done. It's trash, just completely useless, just throw it away."

RE-CHANGES

Another way to kill momentum is to change something and then change it back. I call them "re-changes." It's a rude thing to do. I might say, "I want it like this." So we go and make it like *this*. Then I say, "Oh, but actually you know what, I want it as it was before." Re-changes will kill momentum super-fast because it just made people feel as though they wasted their time.

First of all, I limit re-changes by proper planning. If you absolutely have to do a re-change, try to get your team to come to the conclusion that it's better. It's worth the extra two minutes of guiding the conversation, so they come to the conclusion on their own versus you telling them. It may not work every time but try to get them to say, "Yeah, it was better before. We should move it back." Now, you're not trying to manipulate people, but a real conversation is worth it to try to avoid momentum killing re-changes.

SWING THE MACHETE

Getting stuck in the weeds and worrying about what's going wrong will deflate team spirit. Instead of obsessing over problems, I'll take a step back and return to a project's core goals. These three to five goals are the main objectives we want to accomplish. I'll go back to the "think first" principles that we established.

So I ask myself: "Is there a way to avoid the problem? Is there a way to completely eliminate the problem? Are there ways to defer the decision or the need to address the problem until a later time?" I ask these types of questions as a means to resolve the details and to pull everyone up out of the weeds.

NOTHING PERSONAL

Personal frustrations can also really put a damper on things, especially when they prevent you from giving your team warranted positive feedback. For instance, John comes into the office and is super excited about a feature that he just finished and released into production. Normally you might jump up and down and give high-fives. John would love that and come away from the interaction feeling motivated. But today you have some personal issues on your mind. So, you brush him off. A downer attitude like that can quickly spread from John to the other team members.

I do my best to pay attention when I'm caught up in my own world. As a leader, I can't drag the whole team down due to personal problems. I need to check them at the door accordingly.

UNTIE THE TANGLES & SET THEM FREE

Red tape is another inertia killer that can appear unexpectedly. Sometimes teams are designed with sticking points that cause bottlenecks or feedback delays. These problems are usually easy to identify because people will often start complaining that others are to blame and holding things up.

These bottlenecks might be there by design, by coincidence, or due to restructuring. For example, someone might decide on their own to make decisions that cause delays. The smart manager will always be on the lookout for these obstacles and take fast action to clear the problem.

WHETHER TO HIRE, BUY OR OUTBUILD THEIR COMPETITOR

5

There's a chat service that I really enjoy called Intercom. The company modernized real-time interactions between businesses and their customers, and I've watched them grow from almost nothing to a place where they've started to gain some serious traction.

It's made me wonder a lot about what other larger, established chat systems thought about the appearance of Intercom. Could it be similar to the way Blockbuster viewed Netflix in the early days? In boardroom meetings, were they saying, "These guys are just a fad. We're the 500-pound gorilla in the room. We'll easily outlast them. No big deal."

When I saw Intercom, I knew it was the future, and I knew that they would eat the competition's lunch one day. So in cases like this, should you hire, buy, or outbuild your competitor?

HIRE YOUR COMPETITOR

Hiring your competitor is favorable when you find a product or business at a very early stage. At this stage, the product is likely to be backed only by an individual with a brilliant idea rather than a well-established company. Therefore the potential to fold that individual into your organization is greater. Talk to them. Make an offer to come over and bring their source code. Set-up a nice little package, give them a solid contract, and hire that competitor into your company.

Many businesses are able to do this really well with incubators or startup contests. Here, you'll find a lot of smart entrepreneurial-type developers. Established companies are then able to draw these people into their organization and provide resources that enable them to execute their ideas. These businesses profit off of developer ideas quickly because they are able to leverage company infrastructure (marketing, client base, etc.).

As a result, everybody is happy. The company grows and the developer is equipped with the tools to make his ideas a reality.

BUY YOUR COMPETITOR

Of course, you're not always able to catch sight of the startup when it's just one person. Perhaps the company has already grown from three to ten people before it appears on your radar. In this case, should you outbuild them or buy them?

Let's say the technology is truly disruptive. It makes you say, "Wow! This is the future" when you look at it. If that is the case, I would instantly make the decision to do my due diligence and seek to purchase, even if I needed additional acquisition funding. As long as they pass the due diligence and their technology is stable, it's important to follow your gut feeling. If it's a truly disruptive technology, I'd find a way to buy them. Otherwise I'd drive myself crazy trying to adapt my systems or trying to create a new product team. If the technology is that far off from where I'm at, I would just simply buy them out.

OUTBUILD YOUR COMPETITOR

If purchasing the technology is just not going to happen, I would immediately seek to bring in two or three key individuals that could move us forward. I would look at our code, look at our platform, look at our product, and make a decision. I'd ask myself if this disruption is something we build into our product, or is the technology is so disruptive that it's entirely new.

SUCK IT UP & MAKE A MOVE

Let's return to the Intercom example. There is older customer chat technology that is offered by LivePerson. If I were a company with this older tech, I would've freaked out when I saw Intercom. I would see its potential and start investigating the requirements needed in order to pivot my software. Could my organization find a way to support some of the amazing features, like real time smooth interaction, as well as the backend management features?

The LivePerson systems are older. It would likely be a huge task to pivot and maintain their current operation at the same cost. However, one option available would be to outsource the work to another company that could execute quickly and with a high degree of success. The outsourced company could build an entirely new product. After building the new product LivePerson could start moving people over. They wouldn't have to worry about every piece of data, as their customers only want the new feature. Therefore only the most essential data would need to be migrated.

When you're an established brand in the industry, you have something the startup doesn't—*trust*. Customers that you already have a relationship with will check to see if you have the same capabilities as the lesser known startup before switching. If they're already a fan of your brand, and you support the features they want—or have a product to transition them to that has the features they want—then you will likely keep the customer.

The moment LivePerson loses is when one of their customers notices Intercom and looks to see if Liveperson has the same capabilities. If they don't find what they're looking for, they'll switch. Oftentimes, people will switch because of price or features. If you have a cheaper price and/or better features, people migrate to you.

A FINE KETTLE OF FISH

Don't look now, but there's more. Enter Crisp Chat. This competitor bolted out and quickly spun up their own copy of Intercom and undercut the price big time. Crisp Chat has all of the same features. They look just as pretty, and they're a quarter of the price. Liveperson faces a challenge with Intercom's disruptive technology. But now intercom has to decide how to handle the Crisp Chat price torpedo. How is Intercom going to play this: outbuild, ignore (DON'T!), or buy them?

HOW NOT TO SCALE PREMATURELY

6

There I was, a young developer, suddenly thrust into the role of CTO. Right off the bat, I was given quite the budget. While working with another talented and trusted programmer, I naively handed the reins over to him asking him to hire a bunch of people and assemble a team. We brought about 10 to 15 people on board and began to develop like crazy. Within a month it was an absolute mess.

KEEP THE TEAM TIGHT

Although it's essential to delegate, it's important to establish a structure under which teams are built. First, you need to know how to validate and monitor your leaders. And second, the person that brought you growth may not always be the right person to manage things later. Some people create and some people manage. You can do both, but that's not always the case. It all comes back to the concept of the Modern CTO. Not all developers are built for the job.

In general, I follow these simple guidelines when building teams:

- No more than five in people total, including one to three developers and one to two designers

- Separate the back end from the front end

- Ensure that each team has very specific goals

It turns out that this approach is backed up by data. A QSM study[7] compared large development teams (around 20 people) to small ones (5 people). From start to finish, large teams got things done about a week sooner. However, when you look at cost, big teams spent an average of $1.8M while the small teams only spent $245k. Ouch!

TEAMS ARE LIKE CODE

My teams are structured the way I like to structure code—clean, concise, and with a keenly defined goal. They are small, isolated groups that have a single responsibility. It brings to mind the Law of Demeter,[8] which is an old code that withstood the test of time and still works brilliantly. What makes the Demeter application so resilient? The structure of the code base is small and distributed, and it designates single responsibilities. Development teams thrive under this structure as well.

For example, for large projects I'll break out teams to build iOS, Android, or React Native bindings while other components are being developed by other teams. That way, when the time comes for integration, everything is ready for assembly. I also take leads from the business world in that I have high level leaders, who then manage leaders within smaller teams. This hierarchy sets up a diverse ecosystem, kind of like a rainforest, with each individual component doing its thing to achieve a larger integrated goal.

GROUP REMOTE WORKERS TOGETHER SINCE THEY GET IT

Today's businesses have people located all over the planet working together. How do we handle time zone differences? Here, I've leveraged another key factor—*experience*. By this I don't mean experience measured in years but rather experience working with teams in scattered time zones. It's an acquired skill that those accustomed to working with people in the same time zone are unable to immediately grasp. So I group those working in odd time zones together. I also avoid micromanagement completely. In fact, I only intervene if they don't reach their goals; free-thinking people produce better things faster.

YES, YOU MAY SIT WITH TIMMY

Finally, personality mix is hugely important. As a tech person, it's important to remember that people aren't widgets that work well regardless of where they are plugged in. Move people across teams to find the right combination if needed. Make sure you're constantly scanning for personality conflicts because they often delay progress. Think about it. What makes you more angry at work than anything? It's a person's attitude, right? How much time and energy is wasted fuming over someone that bugs you? I keep my teams lean and harmonious, and we all go home smiling at the end of the day.

HOW TO SOLVE ANY PROBLEM

7

Years ago I watched economics writer, Tim Harford, deliver a TED Talk,[9] and I was blown away by his insight. I realized that I had instinctively been practicing the problem-solving method he described in his talk. But of course, he was able to put it clearly into words.

Tim tells this incredible story about Unilever and the detergent-making nozzle. You see, powdered detergent is made by spraying liquid detergent into the air at a high pressure. The spray dries and becomes powder. It turns out that what determines the quality of the detergent, the most important element of the whole process, is the shape of the nozzle. Now, the nozzle Unilever used to make their detergent was highly inefficient.

UNILEVER HAD A PROBLEM

So what did Unilever do? What problem-solving methodology did they deploy? We encounter problems all the time in our business and personal lives. But if you were to walk up to someone on the street, *Jay Leno style,* and ask what problem-solving tactic he or she would use when encountering a problem, I imagine you'd hear crickets.

THE EXPERT DESIGNED SINGLE SOLUTION METHOD

The Expert Designed Single Solution Method is the most common solution I have seen: "Let's hire an expert, and they will tell us exactly what to do, and it will work the first time." Wrong. Nothing ever works the first time. And Unilever did just that. The company hired some really smart mathematicians and physicists to design a new nozzle. They put a lot of effort into the task, but, despite all their knowledge, the new nozzle produced only mediocre results.

THE TRIAL, ERROR, SELECTION AND VARIATION METHOD

To create a better spray nozzle, the company eventually resorted to a different strategy, the Trial, Error, Selection and Variation Method. In short, they used *science*. First, they made 10 nozzles, more or less at random, and tested them. They kept the nozzle that worked best and made 10 new variations on that winning version. This process of progressive trial and error continued for 45 generations until they created a super nozzle.

What makes this super nozzle so great? They don't know exactly. There was nothing scientifically obvious they could identify that made it better than the others; it just was.

This method works just as well in software development, science, or business as it does in detergent nozzle development. So, when presented with a problem, identify and solve it by trial, error, selection, and a variation of different probable solutions.

Process simplified:

1. Identify the problem.
2. Develop two to three solutions
3. Test the solutions and select the best performing ones.
4. Create variations and repeat.

Sounds simple, right? Well you can apply this to any problem, whether in business, technology, or your personal life. It's really the only way to solve any problem. Most people just get caught up in sticking with the first solution, and they don't complete the cycle.

You can often see the byproduct of sticking with the first solution when you walk into a business and notice something massively illogical. You ask, "Why?" and the answer is, "Well, that's how it's always been."

NEVER FAILS

I like the way Tim ended the talk urging us to step out of our comfort zones, challenge our deepest assumptions, and let the chips fall where they may. In short, don't get into the weeds or get too attached to a particular solution. Instead, work the process. The process works. It always has; it always will; it's *science*.

HOW TO WORK WITH PROGRAMMERS WHEN YOU AREN'T ONE

8

What follows in this section may sound foreign to some readers, but don't skip over it. I consider these my core elements of development success, that is, my *non-negotiables*. Even if you don't understand them, it's important to get familiar with these concepts. I also provide tips on how to manage it all from a high-level perspective.

CREAM OF THE CROP

The top 10-20% of developers have setups that include three essential elements:

- GitHub
- Code Climate
- Continuous Integration

If you or your team are not fluent in these tools and services, then you're not keeping pace with the industry leaders. So get up to speed!

KNOW WHY TESTING MATTERS

One of the most important aspects of development is testing. If testing is not part of the process, it's a warning sign of poor quality. The best developers in the world are also testing experts. If you do not have this knowledge make sure you hire someone who does and avoid hiring anyone who doesn't. If a developer tells you testing will slow the project down, they're probably covering up the fact that they don't know how to test.

MY FIRST BOOK

I remember about a decade ago I read a book for the first time—really. I was in San Francisco working on a project and I had a free afternoon, so I strolled into one of the world's largest bookstores to see what was on the shelves. Before then, I had read maybe two books in their entirety, my whole life. At the store I discovered tons of books about programming written by successful pros that had years of experience. I thought, "Wouldn't it be cool to read every book that exists on Ruby?" So I scooped up all 10 and read them all from cover to cover.

I was blown away by the idea of books and not just books about programming. A book takes an entire person's experience and sums it up in a few hours of reading. A book lays it all out there for you, and you can go back to it again any time you want. The value is incredible. Since then I began to consume books voraciously.

In my course of reading, I learned about testing. Every single great programmer and developer I read about raved about the importance of testing.

TYPES OF TESTING

There are many different types of testing. There's no general consensus about the best type of testing or the timing. I prefer to execute low level model tests—controller testing—and high level integration tests where the features are evaluated regarding their function. That being said, I don't do all three all of the time. Experienced developers will implement testing as they see fit.

It's like going to the gym. There isn't a perfect exercise routine for everyone, but you should definitely work out regularly.

TRAIN, LEARN OR HIRE?

Can you train someone to learn about testing? Yes, but the learning curve is quite steep. While you should educate yourself on the basics, the most practical solution would be to get a testing expert on board sooner than later.

TESTING SAVE TIME AND MONEY

Once you have the tests in place they're useless unless you run them. For example, you might want your code to do A, B, and C. Then a second set of code says, "I want to make sure A, B, and C are working." You run the tests before you deploy your next version of the application.

Two sets of code may sound redundant but in the lifecycle of a project you save time. Plus, the tests are always there and serve as documentation of what the code is supposed to do. You always know the code is working, and passing testing, which increases the intrinsic value of the program. Otherwise, you have to go back into the code to check every single time there might be a problem, which is a big waste of time.

DON'T BE AFRAID OF COMMITMENT

Currently, I use GitHub. It's is a version control repository ("repo") service that uses Git technology to track code versions. Subversion is another service used by many. These services allow you to visualize every line of code and indicate when it was written, and who wrote it.

When using GitHub, you should see frequent "commits" (changes), say every two hours or so. Google's engineers make about 45,000 commits to their repository each day. This record of changes to a file should also be specific. If you see one word commit messages like "update" or something ambiguous there's a problem. Instead, you want something much more detailed like "move exhibits and transitions as inner route switch" or "feat(Global): install ZenDesk widget."

HIGH-LEVEL FOR THE LESS TECH SAVVY

Another great feature of GitHub is that it integrates smoothly with Code Climate. Code Climate allows you to monitor code quality, style, and test coverage for a codebase. The quality of your code, making sure tests are being written, and managing technical debt are items you absolutely need to be aware of.

Another vital tool is Circle CI (Continuous Integration) which determines if your tests are running before being deployed. So you run your tests before things go live.

Again, if you aren't an expert in these tools, hire someone who is. Also, get as familiar with these services as you can. You can start by learning to understand the dashboards.

UX MISTAKES
TO WATCH OUT FOR

9

Remember the user experience (UX) is not just about design. It's about business. UX is just a sliver in the overall process pie. For example, we get caught up in project milestones. Have you ever seen a set of milestones like this:

1. Start UX
2. Finish UX
3. Get first user
4. Get first 100 users

While you may think it's a little bit simplified, I use this strategy all the time. Why? Because it puts the business vision, not the design process, at the forefront.

If you're a developer or manager, you need to think deeply about this. Modern CTOs know all about programming, if they don't, they surround themselves with those who do. As the CTO, you must have a business focus. If this isn't you, that's fine, but don't aspire to something that doesn't fit your personality.

THE PEE TEST

Early on in my programming career, I was highly obsessed with getting my code to run. So much so, that I would be standing there in front of my computer doing the pee dance. If you've ever been really into something and you chose not to go to the bathroom because you were absolutely engrossed in the activity, you understand what I mean. Now obviously, this kind of situation didn't help me focus, and my performance degraded rapidly. #HumanProblems

HUMAN FACTORS ENGINEERING

Human Factors Engineering frequently comes into play in the medical devices field as well as other related industries. It's essentially the concept of making the human-machine interface as friendly as possible. The designers consider things like: "What if the surgeon is tired when using the device?" or, "What happens in a bumpy ambulance ride?" or, "What if the lights go out?" or "How about extremes in temperature or vibration?" I make my apps so easy to use that even during the pee dance, users can make them work.

WHERE DOES THE BUTTON GO?

I've lost count of how many times I've witnessed an argument that goes something like this:

"I think the button should go on the left."
"I think it should go on the right."
"But the left is better. I read about it."
"I disagree. The right makes much more sense."

Then, they just repeat the above four lines over and over again. How do I respond to this? I tell them we'll split test it. I validate that both views have value, and testing will help us decide, but guess what? Ninety-nine-point-nine percent of the time I never do the split testing, and the issue never comes up again.

Why does this happen? People want to be heard. It's not always about power or ego. We, as human beings, need to be heard. Deep down, they really don't care about the button at all. Like birds, we just need to sing sometimes.

THE HALLWAY TEST

The Hallway Test works like this: I test my software on the first random person I encounter that has no vested interest in the project. You want an answer like, "Yeah, whatever. That one's the best." The reason this works is that their response is free of bias and purely practical.

GETTING FEEDBACK

I don't do group user testing. If I ask you to critique something, you'll look for negatives. On the other hand, if I ask you what you love about it, you'll look for positives—but some negatives will slip in anyway. That's why I always ask what they like about something, but I'm very much looking for what they say they *don't* like. It's kind of like the Hallway Test—it's unfiltered feedback. I don't even bother to ask what they "think" about an app. When I ask them to think they get tangled up in a mind game trying to be fair, balanced, or maybe even inoffensive.

SEE IF THEY CAN DO IT

I have a client in the highly specialized field of law. How do I test their app's usability? I give it to a person with no legal background at all and see if they can figure it out. I'll tell my brother-in-law who owns a motorcycle shop, "Hey, check this out. Create a deposition for me." Then I'll watch him scan the screen.

"Oh, here it is," he'll say and click on the *Add Deposition* button. I'll watch him use the application and I'll pick up on intrinsic value through my observation. You see, when people use apps, there's a good chance they're multitasking—at least mentally, so I don't want it to be too complicated. I want it to be simple, easy, and useful.

The point to remember is this—everyone's distracted these days, so I design my applications to deliver the lowest common denominator to fit snugly in the user's world.

PRODUCT DESIGN

Product design isn't a committee process. The truth? I do wireframe designs by myself because if you try to design a horse by committee; you get a camel. I do the wireframing and involve one or two other people (the designer and the developer). I like to collaborate with developers early, so they feel like a part of the process from the get go. They also offer me real-time knowledge, which can circumvent time-killing development snags.

Architects that build buildings have huge amounts of stress and variables swirling around them. They almost always work in very small teams. This structure enables them to deal with new iterations in the most agile manner possible. They've been doing it that way for centuries because it works. That's the kind focus I want to emulate.

CORE GOALS

If you forget everything else in this chapter, remember this: *always return to your core goals.* Your core goals are a list of three to five things your project or product is trying to accomplish. I make sure each core goal has a clearly defined "why?" behind it, this way if I ever get lost, I go back to my "why."

I go off on tangents all the time. I lose my course. That's a normal part of the creative process for me. I need a map to go back to set my ship straight again. Have your core goals prominently displayed.

SUPER CREEPY

What's creep? It's the trap of trying to be everything to everyone. In the business world this means branching out into niches where you can't be successful. In software development, it means losing sight of core goals by trying to be too cute, clever, or complete. I end up adding features that I don't need.

When you go to buy a hammer, you buy a hammer. What if you found a hammer with a first aid kit and flashlight built in? Useless, right? They are better as separate pieces. Although features are harder to visualize as a whole, when it comes to software, the same principle applies.

It's the Law of Diminishing Returns: if you love chocolate ice cream, you'll love it a lot less if you eat it three times a day. Enthusiasm wanes, so we look for something new, even if it's not useful. We end up developing it to death. I've witnessed people become addicted to building technology and the high of the new idea.

The way I avoid this trap is to shift my reward focus. This means I look at milestones that go beyond development. I get my serotonin fix from business milestones instead.

WHEN TO SPEAK UP

10

Loud, smart people are the exception and not the rule. Usually loud people are dumb and quiet people are smart. The *smart/quiet* and *loud/dumb* stereotypes are universally accepted truths. We naturally assume that these go together.

I am constantly filtering messaging from loud people on soap boxes and thinking: "That guy's dumb. That's wrong. That's not even close to the right thing to say." These people come across my path all the time. So when I do find people that say the right thing—guys like Simon Sinek, Elon Musk, or Gary Vaynerchuk—I bring them into my world. I curate my reality and surround myself with their content as a constant reminder that smart and loud is also an option. This way, in my reality, smart and loud become the rule, not the exception.

1000:1

Warren Buffett used to be terrified of speaking in public. He said, "You've got to be able to communicate in life, it's enormously important. Schools to some extent under emphasize that. If you can't communicate and talk to other people and get across your ideas, you're giving up your potential."[10]

Stop for a second and consider your internal dialog—the ideas and thoughts that whiz around your brain. Then, think about what actually comes out of your mouth. See the difference? It might be a ratio of 1000:1 brain to mouth. But, I've learned to bring that ratio down. I discovered that it's okay to take a risk and sound dumb. And you know what? Usually, the only one that thinks you sound dumb is yourself. When you unleash that inner dialog, you become a force to reckon with.

MY DINNER WITH WHARTON GRADS ANECDOTE

One night an investor friend of mine invited me to a Wharton School of Business alumni dinner. It was a small, private event of about 15 people— very fancy. Professor Peter Fader, a major pioneer and voice in the field of customer-centricity was speaking that evening. Customer-centricity stresses the importance of applying data to bring your core clients the most value possible. I ended up sitting next to the guy and engaged him in a conversation.

As the evening passed, I came more and more out of my shell. We shared our MIT experiences and ideas about machine learning, AI, and so on. Then, I made a fatal error. I uttered the word "irregardless." Now there's considerable debate as to whether or not this is even a word. However, at an intimate table of Ivy League grads, surely someone noticed how illiterate I was. Even though I suffered horribly, wishing I could reel that word back into my mouth, I pressed on with the conversation.

Still, being the shy, introverted computer nerd deep down, I was super embarrassed. Under the table, I Googled the heck out of the word trying to justify its use. It took me two days to get over it. Typical, right? You see, as tech-minded people, mistakes are glaring to us. But still, over 80% of my conversation with Professor Fader was amazing.

SUDDENLY, I'M THE EXPERT?

At one point the conversation focused on the fact that Wharton has never received a $100 million donation. Many other Ivy League schools have. In fact, Wharton hasn't even cracked $40 million despite having alumni with that level of giving power. So I'm sitting there listening to this group of Wharton grads lamenting over the situation. Then, I spoke up.

I began to ask questions: "Have you guys analyzed what Harvard and other competitors are doing? What type of content are they putting out and how frequently? Where's the data on messaging and frequency of the material that is getting $100 million donations?"

Wharton has an incredible student body and genius marketing professors. It's a school that educates Fortune 500 execs about business and marketing. It was surprising that they weren't leveraging their skills to solve their own problems. With the best human business and marketing capital in the world on their payroll, they're dripping with resources. Why didn't they bring everyone together to have an hour long meeting about how to get a $100 million donation?

Everyone at the table just stared at me as if to say, "What a novel idea." It was as if this were the first time they heard an idea like this. They said that they didn't know and that the school probably would bring in an outside consultant for this task. I eased up on the conversation after that. I get it; things don't always make sense. I've been called in as a consultant many times. Companies will hire me to look at things, and they won't use their internal resources. Still, if a company specialized in marketing, I doubt they would bring in an outside expert to do their brand marketing for them. You don't see Gary Vaynerchuk hiring a firm to direct his brand; he's the expert. He does it.

It was a disappointment to me that I was able to surprise them. They're the Ivy League for heaven's sake! I was hoping to be schooled. I expected a hot-knife-through-butter response to put me in my place. This story reminds me that we're all just human. Growing up you think all the leaders in this world are really smart and know what they're doing, meanwhile, your life is chaotic. When you get to the top though, you realize that everybody's human. Everyone is just a person.

SHARE YOUR VALUE AT ALL TIMES

Go ahead; take a risk. Israeli judo pioneer and champion, Arik Ze'evi says, "Those close to you will be afraid you'll fail. Others that you'll succeed. Suddenly, you'll see a guy doing exactly what you wanted to do, and it opens up the gate for everyone."[11]

Make friends with people. Help them, even if they're the leaders of your company. Stick next to them, provide them value and they'll pull you up. Remember, there's a beast inside you with a bold internal dialog. Learn to unleash useful information, and people will appreciate it. If you think you have something worthwhile to say, then say it. *Irregardless* of how you imagine they'll react.

HOW TO BE NICE

Now let's say you're the CTO or project manager. When you're the boss, remember this golden rule:

Ask people what they think instead of telling them what to do.

I once had a developer that implemented a validation not included in our project spec. The change came about due to a verbal conversation we had about a business aspect of the project.

To be honest, I was livid when I spotted this. I never asked for the validation. When I went to demo the product, the validation made the demo useless. Thankfully, I resisted the desire to chew him out. Instead, I sent him a message saying, "Hey, I saw the new validation. Interesting, was it in the spec?"

"No. I based it on what you told me the other day," my developer answered.

"Oh, my bad. Thanks." I replied. "You know what? When I demo the product, the validation kind of gets in the way. What do you think, should we write new demo code?"

"No, that doesn't make sense," he answered. "Let's roll back the validation."

See how that works? So instead of being bossy, I used dialog. He was able to express his view, and we came to a consensus with all players intact.

GOOD VIBRATIONS

Now you can be a tyrannical ogre and push projects to completion, but it probably wouldn't be efficient. Happy people, who feel respected, give you their best. Plus, the best talent tends to stick around when the atmosphere is positive and uplifting. Repressed team members will produce only what keeps them out of trouble. Big difference.

So hire people smarter than you are, and let them tell you what to do. #SteveJobs It works like a charm.

WHEN TO
HIRE CONSULTANTS

11

Like any group of people, 80% of consultants are poor-to-average at their work, 19% are decent, and 1% are the cream of the crop.

A BAD TASTE IN MY MOUTH.

In the past, I hated the idea of consultants. A decade ago, I was obsessed with nothing else but writing the best code. Personally, I was ignorant to executive business practices. I thought consultants were useless parasites.

I GREW UP AND LEARNED HOW MUCH I DIDN'T KNOW

You only have to be smart enough to know what you don't know. So 20 projects and a decade later, just like anyone else, I've seen so much more than I can tell. The platforms, the code, the people, business plans, mistakes and successes—it's an absurdly vast collection of experiences stacked up inside me. All the while, I'm playing the selection variation science guy—try this, test, learn, rinse, repeat.

NOW, I HIRE CONSULTANTS

Ever try editing your own writing? It's pretty much impossible. Your eyes adjust and are immune to the mistakes, and they become invisible. That's also what happens when you're tasked with long term projects. If I'm working on miles of code, I need an editor with fresh eyes to review the work and instantly be jarred by what doesn't make sense.

I hire a consultant when I need to tap into a vast network of experience. This could be for a problem or optimization I'm working on. Or maybe it's just for a single project that I'm bored with and need an experienced peer to spice things up. Two great minds collaborating are better than one. I got over my ego, thinking that I can do it all and know it all. Brilliant minds help me get where I want to go faster.

Think about it, you're the only CTO at your company. Competitor CTOs are not the best people to consult. Someone that works with a wide array of CTOs every day may be able to help. This way you tap into a diverse knowledge pool.

HOW TO ANALYZE FAILURE

12

We are judged not by what happens to us, but by how we respond, right?

I've been a part of failed projects. I know how humiliating it is, and how much it hurts. What I've noticed is there's an 80/20 split between how teams respond when things go sour. The 80% I've seen do a failure analysis, figuring out what went wrong. This was my default position too, a habitual post-failure practice. No one taught me this; it was instinctual. Maybe it was culture or society. Maybe it was just me.

It's common to have a what went wrong discussion, but it just reinforces error patterns. Is that what I want?

ONE-EIGHTY

Then, while on a project (after we really botched it), the team talked about what went *right*. It wasn't jarring. In fact, I didn't even notice it really. But later that night in my hotel room, I felt good, energized even. Comparing it with how I normally felt when projects failed, I instantly picked up on the difference. We analyzed what went right, and that left us with a list of strengths to double down on for the next iteration—brilliant.

I intentionally deployed this tactic the next opportunity I had, and it left me feeling good again. Now this is the song I sing all the time: when sh** goes south, double down on what works. Focus on and identify strengths, including who was responsible for what went right.

NOT DENIAL, BUT RIGHT-VISION

Success is built on a collection of failures, but it doesn't drown in failure. I like the method of trial-error-selection-variation, which tries new things and then tries more of what works. It's awesome how this method works in both the scientific and in team processes.

None of this means that I'm blind to mistakes. It's almost like a philosophy about how to address any problem in life. Leave behind the bad, conserve the good, improve, and move on.

HOW TO BOUNCE BACK FROM UNFORESEEN CONSTRAINTS

13

I love unforeseen constraints. Why? Constraints force me to be creative.

When I build a new technology product or work with an entirely new team, ideal results are rare on the first try. It's a process to be worked, not a switch to be flipped. I take a flexible, life-science style approach of trial-error-selection-variation. That way, when unforeseen constraints arise, I adapt and handle them with ease.

POOR PIANO

I've mentioned before that I enjoy Tim Harford's TED talks. In one talk he tells an awesome story about how Vera Brandes, a 17-year-old German concert promoter, set-up a special piano event at the Cologne Opera House. By mistake, a clunker practice piano was provided for the show.

For world renowned jazz musician Keith Jarrett an old, trashy instrument wasn't what he expected at all. Still, he decided to play. He summoned all his determination and creativity out of that beaten down backstage piano. The final outcome was the one of the most famous jazz concerts ever recorded.

As Harford tells it:

"Within moments it became clear that something magical was happening. Jarrett was avoiding the faulty upper registers. He was sticking to the middle tones of the keyboard, which gave the piece a soothing, ambient quality. But also, because the piano was so quiet, he had to set-up these rumbling, repetitive riffs in the bass. And he stood up twisting, pounding down on the keys, desperately trying to create enough volume to reach the people in the back row.

It's an electrifying performance. It somehow has this peaceful quality, and, at the same time, it's full of energy; it's dynamic. And the audience loved it. Audiences continue to love it because the recording of the Köln Concert is the best-selling piano album in history and the best-selling solo jazz album in history."[12]

MINDSET MAKES THE DIFFERENCE

Think about it. Something goes wrong or an unexpected constraint appears. If my reaction is negative, it affects my team and me. But, if I consider the constraint as part of the process, I can step back and look at the problem as an opportunity for creativity.

ANSWER THE QUESTION: "HOW DIFFICULT IS IT TO CODE...?"

14

This question has been my daily reality for 15 years, so I want to talk about it. When it comes to technology, people often ask, "How hard will this be to do?"

When I was a fledgling programmer, I would answer, "It's super easy!" all the time. Why? I wanted to make money and build radical technology. Then, I began to learn about the byproduct of building too much—the dreaded "creep", and creep makes products unusable and unsellable.

There's a reason why there are so many apps in the App Store. People mentally associate apps with a specific use. Go beyond that primary use and two things happen (and both hurt you).

DING

#1 – Your app becomes too complicated to explain. People share, people talk about what they do, and talking about a new app is no exception. The easier it is for them to relay your message the more viral your product will be.

Look at the human attention span and the forgetting curve. Better yet, look at how politicians speak at a third grade reading level, and it isn't because Americans are stupid. It's because *simple spreads*. It's the reason why company taglines are short and sweet. Ambiguity frees us to apply our own meaning.

DING DING

#2 – The more complicated the app; the harder it is to sell. A knife is simple. It's used to cut things. The decision is clear. If I want to cut something, I need a knife. Learning to design my technology this way has proven to be critical.

Once I developed an entire creep-filled real estate platform that could do A–Z and required a three week training program. This was an expensive lesson to say the least.

PUNCH BACK

One neat trick I learned was to develop the sales page for the product first. It helps me to focus on the customer and deliver the features that would interest them. Try to solve too many problems and well…that hammer radio flashlight combo didn't sell too well, did it?

HOW I RESPOND NOW

Today when I'm asked how hard it will be, I still respond optimistically. Then I go do the research and figure it out. I think about the time and resources I'll need. Most importantly, I determine if what I'm being asked to do will add value to the customer. If it doesn't fit, don't build it. A shiny new idea with a hollow core devours a budget, kills business, and leaves you holding the bag. There's always plenty to do to move the simple product forward in a meaningful way.

HOW TO AVOID THE "BOTTOM OF THE NINTH GUY"

15

L et's call him Voldemort because, well, I can't use his real name. It's not really one person at all. It's more a collection of recurring red flag personalities I've encountered repeatedly. Let's examine these traits in people that I try to avoid.

THE "WEARS MANY HATS" GUY

He's always busy and gets nothing done. When you ask what this guy has accomplished, you'll get a lot of words but no tangible, needle-moving value. If I hear someone repeatedly saying the phrase 'wears many hats', I instantly begin a mental value audit and ask questions like:

- What high-level goals are you working on this week to push business forward?

- Can you pull-up last week's accomplishments?

Ten times out of ten, I'll get a deer-in-the-headlights stare. Around the third time I encountered this Voldemort, I realized the phrase 'wears many hats' really means 'help, I don't know what I'm doing'.

These people might just need a bit of guidance. If it were me, maybe I would try to recommend a book or website about how to organize objectives to move business forward. I'd try to give them a chance to learn some new skills, and they just might begin to add real value. Then, I'd move along and put the focus back onto actual objectives and goals.

THE "BOTTOM OF THE NINTH" GUY

I've seen horrific scenarios, due to pure laziness, that create the perfect storm just so that this guy can come and "save" the day. This individual boasts about last minute, total chaos, we-barely-made-it stories, regularly, And is *proud of them*.

People are a byproduct of their environment. A person with an endless repository of *saved the day stories* is always involved in dysfunctional situations. Do I want that person on my team?

GUY WHO KNOWS EVERYTHING ABOUT EVERYTHING AND NEVER STOPS TALKING

How can you learn anything if you never stop talking? Quiet people are the smartest people I know, probably because they're expert listeners. They're the ones with a strong wisdom cortex. Still, if you have something worthwhile to say, speak up. Being an introvert is not the same as being wise.

If you think about it, listening requires you to hold back, pay attention, process, and understand. The more you do this, the greater capacity for patience you'll have, and the patience you develop can be used to learn more. It's a positive feedback loop.

A MODERN CTO KNOWS...

WHEN TO ABANDON SHIP

16

About 80% of my projects are failed takeovers. I've come into companies that were $700K in the hole, sitting on a giant mess. I often ask myself these questions: "Should I try to repair their broken codebase? Is it worth trimming the fat and doing my best with what's left over?" And I make a decision based on several key factors.

CODE QUALITY

What's the quality of the code and test coverage? Is it long spaghetti code or short, tight classes? I'll take a look at the sections of code that programmers avoid like the plague. I'll ask, "How hard is it to make minor adjustments or debug?" Keep your eyes peeled for the Spaghetti Triangle. Like the Bermuda Triangle, it makes time, money, and resources vanish into thin air. You might want to jump ship here.

CUSTOMER-CENTRICITY

How far off are the application's features from the business goals? Is it drowning in creep and over-engineering? How many features does your application have? How many are satisfying customer needs? This pairing should be direct, easy to understand, and demonstrable.

I'd also ask what kind of feedback has been gathered and take a look at it. Have the users responded at all? Have the programmers made knee-jerk feature changes? Or did they wait for significant feedback numbers and then make wise, limited modifications?

TEAM COMPOSITION

Who's on the team? Are they an A-team or a B-team? For example, I look for boomerang players. By this I mean someone you send out on a task, and they come back with it finished. I shouldn't have to monitor and chase them all the time.

When I'm called in to evaluate a project, I take the pulse of the team. How's morale? Is everybody upbeat, or are they miserable? Are people collaborating in a fluid way, or are they stubborn and isolated? No matter how great their tech skills are, if team members hate each other, things don't go well for the business.

It's also important to consider team structure and composition. I'll look at personality types, leadership skills, relationships, coding abilities, and evaluate how these factors unify or divide the team. When things are bad, it's palpable. The best teams have a cheerful balance.

In the past, I've completely missed the boat. I only looked at things from the technical aspect and failed to consider the human element. If I can't asses the human component, I can't lead a team. For the CTO it's a critical skill. Team composition carries as much or perhaps even greater weight than programming expertise.

MAKE THE DECISION

Finally, the decision arises between salvaging the old system or writing a new simple system from scratch. The reality? Nine times out of ten, what I encounter is unacceptable, and it's time to abandon ship and build a new one. However, it takes a while to get motivated enough, (or scared enough) to address the problem. By the time I'm called in, it's usually a long-standing issue, and I'm just there to confirm and triage. I'm amazed at how many companies let it get so far out of control—deep pockets, I guess.

In the long run, it will usually cost more to fix a broken system than to build new one. Plus, I can stand behind the new system since I know it was built properly from the start.

OWN IT

If you're sitting on a situation like this in your organization, ask yourself if you should build a better ship. If you're unsure, bring in an expert. Don't just keep a faulty project rolling until things blow up, or until shareholders ask why a project costs so much but delivers so little. If you stand there and watch it bleed, you're responsible. If you reach out and stop the bleeding, you're the hero.

HOW TO MISS A DEADLINE

17

Remember the old days when you had to ship physical packages to customers in a CD format? A different version came out every 6-12 months. It was a big deal with a big buildup of features and changes in a single release. Now the landscape looks much different. With continuous integration, we push changes and updates all the time. There's less build up and more focus on rapid deployment and improvement.

COMING NEXT SUMMER...

There are times that I'll still have to schedule a release—for instance to meet shareholder expectations, for a large revision, or for the development of a totally new product. In those situations, I'll factor in a 20% margin for timelines and schedule the release by season. Doing this frees me from a looming public due date and gives me the freedom of a three month buffer instead.

My preference, though, is to regularly push changes, so a big build-up is avoided when possible. But if I'm doing a whole new rewrite, I'll do it by season/quarter.

IT'S ALL ON ME

What's the best way to hit or beat your deadline? *Get the best people.* You only want people on board with exceptional skills and motivation. If necessary, bring in experts and consultants. Don't know who they are? Ask around. Get a personal recommendation on someone who's done stellar work. Great ideas and management won't take you very far if you don't have the team to carry out the plan.

The B-Team gets B results, but the A-Team gets A results. Don't want to build it internally? Then, go out and get it. Hire or outsource the people that will get the job done. As CTO, I'm ultimately responsible for anything that happens in the technology. I get to point zero fingers. And what's the CEO thinking if things go south? She is thinking, "It's my fault since I hired this CTO that failed."

Pause and consider that for a second. The CEO feels like a failure for hiring you. That's brutal. Now flip it over. What if the CEO feels like a genius and a hero for hiring you? Let this be your motivation for assembling a superlative team.

SIMPLY BETTER

Next, it's critical to consider the most minimally viable lifecycle. I do this by starting with the most basic implementation of a feature. Then I rapidly release updates. Let's say I want my app to do text messaging. So with my first release, I won't roll out a snazzy GIF keyboard. Instead, I'll build a rock solid, basic end-to-end messaging platform. I'll establish and nail down one goal. Now, my team, my shareholders, and I are all satisfied.

I'M NOT DONE YET

If I start with a really easy and basic app, then I deal with a small set of issues with each update. My timeline becomes more predictable. Compare this with trying to build a massive production application that may be ready and working locally, but when it goes to production there are 70 production-related issues to fix.

In other words, when I'm sitting at my computer everything may work smoothly, but in order to put it into production, I may need to deal with an entirely new set of issues that could arise. I used to think I was done when I completed staging, but I was wrong. It's *done* when the application is fully operational in production. As a leader, it's important to think from a non-technical perspective. *Done* means that it's done from the perspective of the end user.

KEEP MOMENTUM GOING

Instead of accumulating a ton of work in a massive staging process, I put out the very first basic version into production. It's neat, clean, and fully functioning. In a similar fashion, I roll out all updates directly into production too. I don't try to do it all at once. Instead, with this step-by-step strategy, I'm constantly releasing fully operational products and updates.

I try to make it simple and beautiful, but I don't use simplicity as an excuse to cut corners. When I limit my focus and scope, I'll produce excellent UX. If you consistently hit small goals, you set up a string of victories that keep momentum going.

WHEN TO RESPOND
TO FEEDBACK

18

So you're a developer or a software company, and you made a great tool that doesn't exist. It blew everyone's mind. Suddenly, two customers appear complaining that they want this or that, and you're freaking out. It's okay. Nothing will be perfect for everyone. Don't become a contractor for individual customers.

YOU WANT VOLUMINOUS FEEDBACK

Avoid the knee jerk reaction to act on feedback from the first few users. Here's how I do it instead. I wait for feedback from 100 people before adjusting. It's important to keep in mind that you're not building for one person but for a collective group of people. When listening to the feedback, you'll notice two to three items requested over and over again. It's almost as if you don't need to write them down because everyone says the same thing. These are the items to focus on in the next release.

IT MATTERS HOW YOU ASK

When receiving feedback, the method I prefer is asking what they *like* about the application. When you analyze the feedback, though, look for what they say they *don't like*. This is where you can add value. Still, don't specifically ask for negatives. When asking for positives, if criticism appears, it's something that really bothered them. If you ask for a critique, they search out the negatives, which might not be that important.

ONE FOOT, THEN THE OTHER

The feedback process becomes unfocused if you try to change too much at once. In scientific experiments, if you modify too many variables, the data gets too noisy to get any real meaning. So I'll change only the most requested items that bring the most value to the most people. After the next release, I'll ask for feedback again.

PERSONAS ARE PEOPLE

Although personas are an abstract representation of a group of people, I'll make sure to get to know real people that represent the persona. For example, if I'm working on an app for attorneys, I'll get to know an actual trial attorney, corporate lawyer, personal injury lawyer, etc. That way, if I'm looking for specific input on something, like a new transcriptions feature, I have a real person I can ask. Since I'm not an attorney, there's no way I can see things from their point of view. I leverage my resources to build the best product, and their experience is a valuable resource.

HOW TO VALIDATE
AN EXPERT IN ANY FIELD

19

can't know everything, so I often need to bring experts on board. Many people have asked me for a way to validate experts. *How do you see through the smoke?* So, I started paying attention, and here's what I learned.

Let's say I have to hire someone for an AI specialty task about which I know nothing. First, I do some basic research and find terms that are unknown to me. Then I backfill my knowledge gaps, the things I don't know that stand out. Like, what's "gradient descent" or "linear regressions?" Something that may sound absurdly complicated, can actually be something very simple. When I interview the candidate, I'll ask for an explanation of the term. If I get a clear answer in simple terms, then I'm probably talking to a non-idiot, which is an excellent start.

CAN'T FAKE IT

If the candidate stutters around and reaches to make something up, I notice. Reaching is different from not knowing, and I'm not sure how to express the difference in words, but I can feel it. If they don't know and say, "Hey, I'm not sure, but this is what I do know. This is what I'm aware of…." Now, that's professional. The medical consultant that never admits knowledge gaps can be very dangerous to patient outcomes.

If a candidate can explain the path of progress simply, that's what I'm looking for. At some point, I'll challenge them to go deeper. They should have a firm grasp on all parts of the plan. If not, they haven't done it before.

FEYNMAN TECHNIQUE

Richard Feynman won the Nobel Prize in physics. Albert Einstein and Bill Gates are considered some of Feynman's biggest fans. He's been referred to as the *Great Explainer*. How did this intellectual giant explain things?

As if he were teaching a child. He dedicated his whole life to explaining complex things simply. He mastered the skill and labelled it the "Feynman Technique."[13] When I came across this term, I was surprised because it was what I had been doing. I even had my own term for it which I called "Reduce, Refine, Repeat."

WHAT DO I SAY?

As an expert, I've been validated tons of times. While sitting in a board room full of experts in their own fields, the grilling begins. If someone is validating me, they're thinking, "Do I want to take this guy to the ball?" And so the dance begins. In some cases, they might just ask me what I would do about a certain application. If it's a vague *rewrite-a-system* process inquiry, my response might sound like this:

> "First, I'll check how well the business objectives line up with your code. Are there 20 different features, but only one truly benefits your business? If so, we've identified bloat, technical debt, lack of customer centricity, or a number of other words that mean the same thing—bad code. After comparing the source code to business goals, I'll help you decide whether to rebuild or continue with what you have. Then, we'll set up a roadmap, a week-by-week plan. I'll provide you with constant updates, and you'll sign off on everything. Don't know much about testing? We'll it's really important, and I can show you how to monitor it easily.

> I've been writing code for 17 years. I only work with, and have, the best people on my teams. I know exactly what I'm asking people to do, how long it should take them to do it, and how to evaluate quality...."

AND SO ON...

You see, I can explain it forever in an easy-to-understand manner. The reality is that I typically only get a quarter of the way through my monologue before questions come up. I have no problem getting interrupted to drill down into detail. I give them a full menu of topics from which to choose, and the answers get served up piping hot.

EXPERTS LOVE BEING VALIDATED

The other day I had a guy come over to my home to fix a gas leak. While we walked around the house, I peppered him with questions to validate him. The guy just oozed knowledge about his trade, and he even looked the part in his overalls and all. He could talk about gas lines and ovens all day without missing a beat. There was no doubt the man was an expert.

Watch how smoothly they respond. Give them a platform to share their experience. If they get defensive, they're hiding holes in their experience. If they respond with passion, enthusiasm, and an abundance of knowledge, then you've got your expert.

HOW TO
EFFECTIVELY COMMUNICATE
COMPLEX IDEAS

20

t happens all too often. I see investors come in and steal the credit from brilliant technologists who failed to communicate the value of their tech. Is this really stealing though? How much is good communication worth? Millions.

If I have a new tool and I want to protect my equity, I'd better be able to:

- Clearly explain how it works (Can I explain it to a child?)

- Fluently answer questions on market potential

- Navigate my way through my first customers

- Fully understand funding: seed (friends and family), angel, venture capital, mezzanine (if I'm taking the financing route)

What sits at the heart of all this? Value communication. That's what investors do. They communicate value within their circles to raise money. The more room you give to investors to develop resources, the more value you hand over to them.

A CHIMP COULD UNDERSTAND IT

My communication method is "Reduce, Refine, Repeat." It's like I toggle back and forth from the *primitive ape me* and the *highly intellectual me* until the ideas gel into one.

I continuously make things simpler. I'm going to spoon feed lobster to the king, so the client doesn't have to crack it apart piece by piece. If I spoon feed, I'll have the king's favor. The easier I make something to understand, the more people will spread the word. Why do politicians speak at a third grade level? Simple spreads.

THIS SKILL MAKES YOU MONEY

Remember the Feynman Technique? The best way to explain complex ideas is with brief and simple terms. If you can't do this, then you don't understand the topic.

As CTO, if you can't explain value simply, it means you don't understand the business value behind your technology. It doesn't matter if you understand it internally. If you can't communicate it simply to the outside world, you don't understand. A savvy investor, however, will pick out the value in a heartbeat. Ultimately, you'll pay for their ability to effectively communicate the value of what you are doing.

I DO IT FOR ME

I make things simple for my own benefit, so I can get a handle on what I'm doing. Simplicity lets me understand the *why*. It keeps the business value of any system I build in front of me at all times.

However, simplifying things has led to some unintended benefits. I practiced this skill for my own benefit, but it brought a greater value than just my ability to write clean code to the business. I was called in for quality code for industries ranging from Bitcoin, to real estate, to law. Then, I ended up taking a seat at the table. Why? All business is a value exchange, and I speak value. Now, people approach me to provide simplicity and value, and the code part ends up being secondary, if coding is involved at all. Isn't life interesting?

ENDNOTES

1   Julie Bort. "You Can Learn To Be The Next Steve Jobs: Nine Ways To Become A Million Dollar Visionary." *Business Insider,* last modified May 1, 2012. www.businessinsider.com/you-can-learn-to-be-the-next-steve-jobs-nine-ways-to-become-a-million-dollar-visionary-2012-4.

2   Simon Sinek, "12 Lessons: Start With Why" *Block-shelf.com,* last modified March 17, 2015 http://www.blockshelf.com/start-with-why/

3   Peter F. Druker, *The Effective Executive* (HarperCollins e-books, 2009), Kindle edition.

4   Elon Musk, "Acronyms Seriously Suck." Email. May 2010 quoted in Klaas Pieter Annema, "Acronyms Seriously Suck - Elon Musk" *GitHubGist.com*, last modified June 22, 2017. https://gist.github.com/klaaspieter/12cd68f54bb71a3940eae5cdd4ea1764

5   Bill Nye, *Undeniable: Evolution and the Science of Creation, 1st Edition.* (St. Martin's Press, 2014)

6   Interview by Kevin Rose, "The First Principles Method Explained by Elon Musk" YouTube video, 2:48, posted by "innomind," December 4, 2013. https://www.youtube.com/watch?v=NV3sBlRgzTI

7   "Haste Makes Waste When You Over-Staff to Achieve Schedule Compression" *QSM, last modified February 18, 2016. http://www.qsm.com/risk_02.html*

8   Robert Brautigam, "The Genius of the Law of Demeter" *DZone/Java Zone, last modified May 16, 2017. www.dzone.com/articles/the-genius-of-the-law-of-demeter*

9   Tim Hartford, "Trial, error and the God complex," *TED Talks video, 18:00, July 2011. https://www.ted.com/talks/tim_harford*

10   Carmine Gallo, "How Warren Buffett and Joel Osteen Conquered Their Terrifying Fear of Public Speaking" *Forbes, last modified May 16, 2013. www.forbes.com/sites/carminegallo/2013/05/16/how-warren-buffett-and-joel-osteen-conquered-their-terrifying-fear-of-public-speaking/#66758a08704a*

11   Arik Zeevi, "Personal growth through risk taking Arik Zeevi at TEDxIDC," YouTube video, 9:57, posted by "TEDx Talks," December 10, 2013, from http://www.youtube.com/watch?v=_dRq_qYxmCI.

12 Tim Hartford, "How frustration can make us more creative," TED Talks video, 15:33, September 2015. https://www.ted.com/talks/tim_harford_how_messy_problems_can_inspire_creativity

13 "Learning From the Feynman Technique" *Medium.com*, last modified August 4, 2017. https://medium.com/taking-note/learning-from-the-feynman-technique-5373014ad230

Made in the USA
Coppell, TX
08 May 2021